Jolly Meets Cyber Air Bully

By: Brucetta McClue Tate, Ph.D.

AuthorHouse™
1663 Liberty Drive
Bloomington, IN 47403
www.authorhouse.com
Phone: 1 (800) 839-8640

Because of the dynamic nature of the Internet, any web addresses or links contained in this book may have changed
since publication and may no longer be valid. The views expressed in this work are solely those of the author and do not
necessarily reflect the views of the publisher, and the publisher hereby disclaims any responsibility for them.

Any people depicted in stock imagery provided by Getty Images are models,
and such images are being used for illustrative purposes only.
Certain stock imagery © Getty Images.

This book is printed on acid-free paper.

ISBN: 978-1-4685-8719-7 (sc)
ISBN: 978-1-4772-3365-8 (e)

Library of Congress Control Number: 2012907282

Print information available on the last page.

Published by AuthorHouse 07/11/2020

authorHOUSE®

"Hi Jumpy and Jana it is been some months since we have seen each other."

"Yes, Jolly how have you been?"

"Oh, Jumpy it has been a toughie nine months."

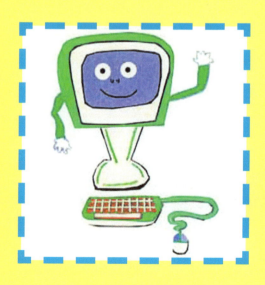

My system has been upgraded many times. I cannot keep up with the technology boom.

"Oh Jolly you are a smart guy and no one can ever case what the Greeks are thinking. Who are the Greeks? They are the smart people and the ones that go to school and learn."

"When was the last time you saw the parts of the computer?" said Jana. "Oh, I have not seen the parts for over seven months. I wonder if they would like to come over," said Jana. "So call them and ask them said jumpy."
RING, RING, RING

"Hi everyone this is Jana. Would you like to come and sit with us today?" "Sure," said Towner the CPU;

"Sure," said All-Around Software;

"Sure," said Fly the headphones;

"Sure," said Gray the keyboard;

"Sure," said Green the printer;

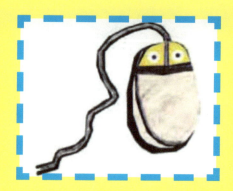

"Sure," said Gray Mousy Mouse;

"Sure," said White the DVD;

"Sure," Said Yellow the scanner;

"Sure," said Black the cable;

"Sure," said Brown USBesty!

"Well, Jolly, Jumpy, and Jana How are you doing?"
All the parts giggle at one time.

"I am doing great," giggled Jumpy.
Jolly and Jana just waved their
hands.

"Well, since the last time we have seen you guys we have been pushed around by a virtual cyber problems in our computer world."

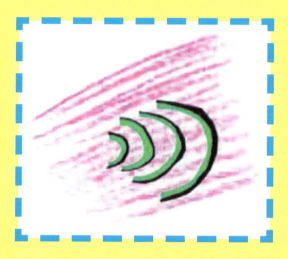

"Every time we turn on one of our parts to help a student, a computer terrible cyber pops-up and calls us bad names and threatens us."

"Who is it, Green the Printer?" asked Jolly.
"They call him 'Cyber Air Bully.'"

"Cyber Air Bully? Where did he come from?"

said White the DVD.

"Oh Jumpy, he is new on the internet and he is not very friendly at all."

"He stops many of the children from coming and learning on the social networks, which is a good quality place to get information."

"Oh Jana, he is such a terrible person. He has turned what is good into bad."

"Well," said Jolly. "I guess I will have to find Mr. Cyber Air Bully and teach him a good lesson on respect."

"Oh Jolly would you, would you, could you, could you….." "Yes, everyone do not worry. I will find Cyber Air Bully and teach him a good computer message. I could, I would stop and purge him from the social network."

"Jolly, Jolly, Jolly be careful he is a mean one and Cyber Air Bully does not play." "Oh do not worry!"

Yellow the Scanner said,  "Cyber Air Bully has not met Jolly yet."

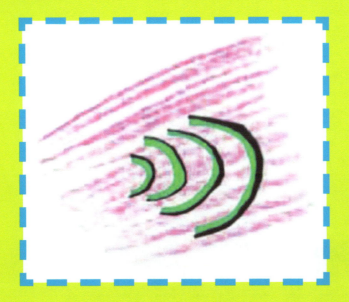

"Where are you going Jolly?" they all shouted out. "I am going to the room to login the computer so I can meet 'Cyber Air Bully'."

"Be careful Jolly," said Yellow the Scanner.

"I will guys. Do not worry," shouted Jolly.   Jolly login and he waited and waited and waited and waited. He typed in the computer "Hi I am Jolly, and I would like to learn more about Cyber Air Bully".

Suddenly, Cyber Air Bully answers.

"Hi I am Cyber Air Bully and you are a smart one." Jolly said, "Yes, smarter than you." "So you think your smarter than I?" giggles Cyber Air Bully, chuckle, chuckle........Jolly said," Cyber Air Bully, why are you frightening my friends.?"

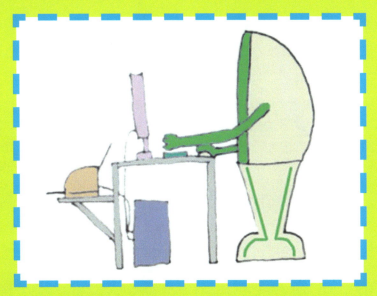

"Why are you bullying them every time they login?"
"I am Cyber Air Bully, and I rule the internet world,"
he said. "I come in your social network, and I steal all
your information." HA,HA, laughed Cyber Air Bully.
"You cannot stop me."

Jolly said, "Cyber, Cyber, I am not scared of you. I
am asking that you stop scaring the children that
use the internet. The internet is a good tool to help
them with their school work and social network with
their friends. It is not suppose to be a scary place, but
an information world for positive learning. Do you
understand Mr. Cyber Bully?"

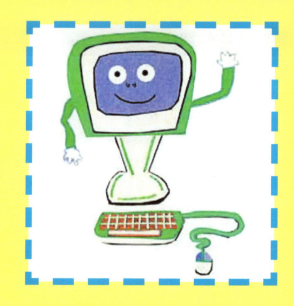

"Stop, stop, stop Cyber Air! Do you hear me? Stop it now.!" "Jolly, Jolly, do you know who I am? I will scare you right out of here. Where do you live Jolly? What is your phone number Jolly? What school do you go to Jolly? Tell me, tell me, tell me what school you go to Jolly tell me, tell me, tell me...? "No, no Cyber Air Bully I will not give you that information so that you can hurt me. No, no, no Cyber Air Bully."

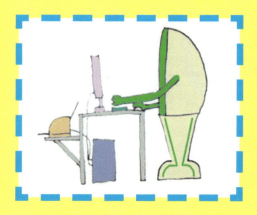

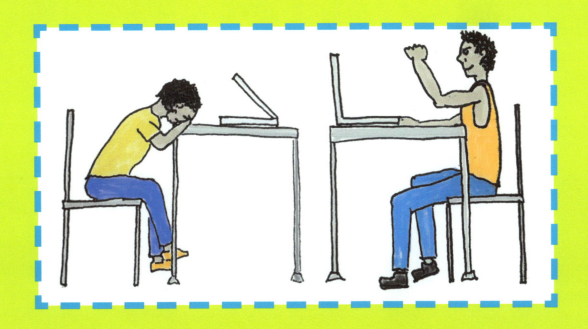

"Okay Jolly, I will find out anyway. I can see you from
the other end." Jolly turned off his webcam.   Cyber
Air Bully said, "Come back, come back, come back!"
Jolly typed in the computer" keep typing Cyber Air
Bully and I will beat you.

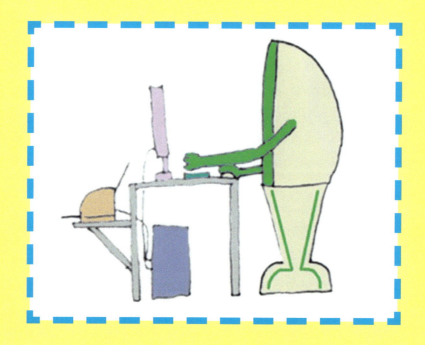

Jolly called his parents and told them what was going on. Jolly's parents called the bully hot line number while logged in the computer. The Cyber police logged in, and found Cyber Air Bully's address.

Jolly said, "Bye-bye, by Cyber Air Bully." Cyber Air
Bully said, "I will get you Jolly when you log back in."
Jolly said, "We will see about that Cyber Air Bully."
"Are you threatening me, Jolly?" said Cyber Air.

Jolly said, "No, I am just smarter than you!" Cyber Air Bully said, "Wait Jolly someone's at my door." Cyber Air Bully went to the door, and Cyber officer read Cyber Air Bully his internet rights in front of his parents. Cyber Air Bully loss his entire rights to the internet. Cyber Air shouted, "I will get you Jolly! I will get you..." The Cyber police took him away to the Cyber Bully Learn to Do Right Academy.

Jolly went back in the room.

Jumpy, Jana, and the parts of the computer smiled, and said, "Oh Jolly are you alright?" "Yes, guys I am alright," whispered Jolly. "Oh, Jolly you are our fearless friend and hero."

UBesty said, "Get some rest Jolly."
Jolly said, "Sure guys, I have saved the internet world, and we all can access the internet and our social groups without being scared." "Jolly come see us at the school sometimes." "I will USBesty, I will."

Spanish
Versión Española

Jolly Cumple Cibernético Air Bully

POR: Brucetta McClue Tate, Ph.D.

Hola Jumpy y Jana se fue unos meses desde que se han visto

Sí, Jolly ¿cómo has estado?

Oh, Jumpy ha sido una decisión difícil de nueve meses.

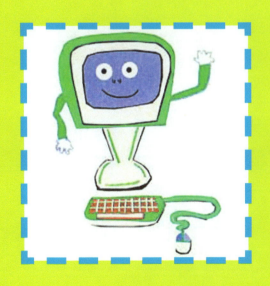

Mi sistema se ha actualizado muchas veces. No puedo seguir con el auge de la tecnología.

Oh Jolly usted es un hombre inteligente y nadie puede caso, lo que los griegos están pensando. ¿Quiénes son los griegos? Son las personas inteligentes y las que van a la escuela y aprender.

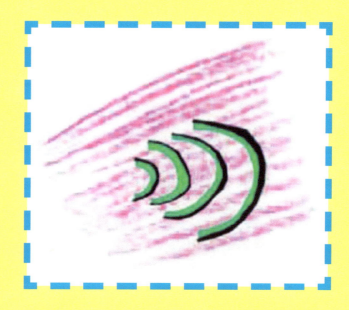

¿Cuándo fue la última vez que has visto las partes de la computadora, dijo Jana. ¡Oh, no he visto las piezas de más de siete meses. Me pregunto si les gustaría que viniera, dijo Jana. Llame a ellos y preguntarles, dijo nervioso. RING, RING, RING

Hola a todos este es Jana le gustaría venir y sentarse con nosotros hoy? Claro dijo Towner, la CPU

 Claro, dijo All-Around de software

Claro, dijo, Vuela de los auriculares

Claro, dijo Gray, el teclado

Claro, dijo Green, la impresora.

Claro, dijo el ratón Laucha Gray

Claro, dijo White, el DVD,

Claro dijo Amarillo, el escáner

Claro dijo el Negro, el cable no se puede por cable;

Claro, dijo Brown USBesty

Bueno, Jolly, Jumpy, y Jana ¿Cómo estás? Todas las partes risita al mismo tiempo.

Estoy haciendo reír Jumpy grande. Jolly y Jana sólo agitaban sus manos.

Pues bien, desde la última vez que le hemos visto a tipos que han sido empujado por un ciber virtual, causando problemas en nuestro mundo de la informática.

Cada vez que encendemos nuestra parte para ayudar al estudiante a una computadora horrible ciber pops-up y nos llama malos nombres y nos amenaza.

¿Quién es el verde de la impresora? Ellos lo llaman "Cyber Bully

Aérea".

Ciber Bully Aire donde ha salido el DVD de White? Oh, Jumpy, que es nuevo en Internet y no es muy amable en todas.

Se detiene a muchos de los que los niños entren y aprendizaje en las redes sociales que es un lugar de buena calidad para obtener información.

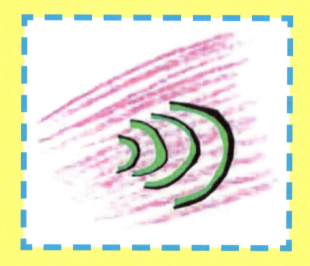

Oh, Jana, que es una persona tan terrible. Ha convertir lo que es bueno en malo. Bueno, dijo Jolly Supongo que tendrá que encontrar al señor de Cyber Bully aire y le daré una buena lección en el respeto.

¡Oh alegre que lo haría, ¿verdad, podría usted, usted podría ..... Sí, todo el mundo no te preocupes. Voy a encontrar Cyber Bully aire y enseñarle un mensaje del equipo bueno. Pude, me detenía y purgar él desde la red social.

Jolly Jolly Jolly tener cuidado de que es un medio y Cyber Bully un aire no se reproduce. Oh, no te preocupes

Amarillo el escáner de  Cyber Bully aire no ha cumplido con Jolly.

¿A dónde vas «Jolly» todos gritaron a cabo? Voy a la sala para entrar en el equipo

Para que yo pueda cumplir con Cyber Bully aire. Un cuidado Jolly dijo Amarillo del escáner.

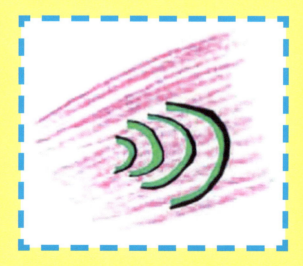

Voy a chicos que no se preocupe, le gritó Jolly. De inicio de sesión Jolly y esperó y esperó y esperó y esperó. Él escribe en la computadora "Hola, soy alegre y me gusta aprender más acerca de Cyber Bully Aire».

De repente, ciber Aire respuestas Bully. "Hola soy de Cyber Bully aire y usted es uno inteligente.» Jolly, dijo que sí más inteligente que tú. Así que usted piensa que su risa más inteligente que yo, Cyber Bully aire, se ríen, se ríen .... Jolly, dijo Cibernético Bully aire, ¿por qué usted está asustando a mis amigos.

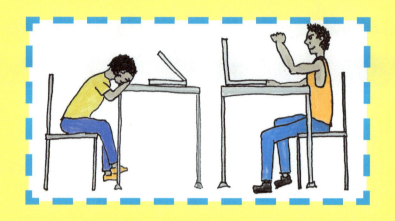

¿Por qué ellos la intimidación cada vez que ingresa al sistema? Yo soy de Cyber Bully aire, y gobernar el mundo de Internet, dijo. Yo vengo en su red social, y robo toda su información. Ja, ja, se rió de Cyber Bully aire que no me puede detener. Jolly dijo, Cyber, Cyber, yo no tengo miedo de ti. Estoy pidiendo que usted deja de asustar a los niños que utilizan internet. El Internet es una buena herramienta para ayudarles con sus tareas escolares y de la red social con sus amigos. No se supone que debe ser un lugar de miedo, pero un mundo de información para el aprendizaje positivo. ¿Entiende el Sr. Cyber Bully?

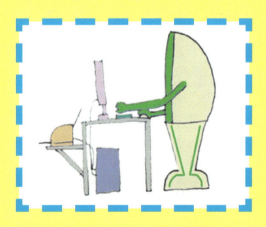

Parar, parar, parar aire cibernético, ¿me oyes me detenerlo ahora. Jolly Jolly, ¿sabe usted quién soy yo? Yo te asusta nada más sacarlo de aquí. ¿Dónde vive usted Jolly? ¿Cuál es su número de teléfono Jolly? ¿A qué escuela vas a Jolly? Dime, dime, dime a qué escuela vas a Jolly dime, dime, dime ... ? No, no Cyber Bully aire no voy a dar esa información para que pueda hacerme daño. No, No, No Cyber Bully aire.

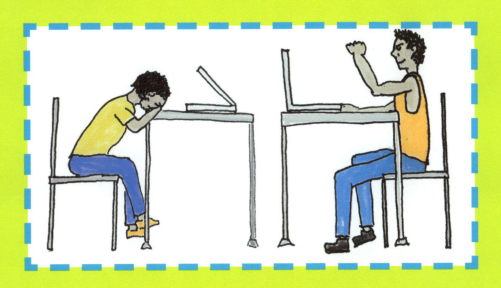

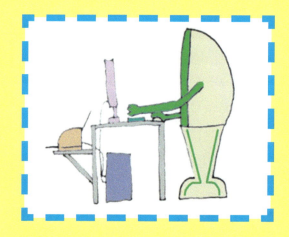

Bueno Jolly, voy a averiguar de todos modos. Te puedo ver desde el otro extremo. Jolly apagó la cámara web.

Ciber Aire Bully dijo volver, volver, volver, tipo de Jolly en el ordenador siga escribiendo de Cyber Bully aire y te golpearé. Jolly llamó a sus padres y les contó lo que estaba pasando. Los padres Jolly llamó al número de matón de la línea caliente mientras está conectado al ordenador. El inicio de sesión la policía cibernética, y se encontró la dirección cibernética del aire de matón.

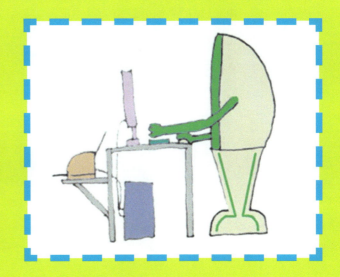

Jolly dijo que por Cyber Bully aire.
Ciber Aire Bully dijo que le dará
Jolly cuando al iniciar sesión con Facebook Jolly dijo
que lo veremos Cyber Bully aire. ¿Me está amenazando
Jolly dijo Cibernético de aire?

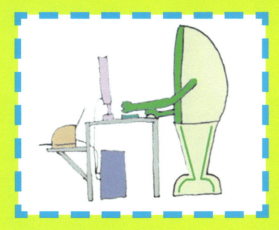

Jolly dijo que no acabo de forma más inteligente que tú. Ciber Aire Bully, dijo esperar que alguien alegre que está en mi puerta. Ciber Aire Bully fue a la puerta, y Cyber oficina de lectura de Cyber Bully aire sus derechos en internet frente a sus padres. Ciber pérdida Bully aire sus derechos completos a Internet.

Ciber Aire gritó voy a tener que Jolly, te voy a conseguir ... La policía cibernética le llevó hasta el Cyber Bully Aprendamos a hacer el Derecho de la Academia.

Jolly volvió en la habitación, Jumpy, Jana, y las partes de la computadora sonrió y dijo: oh Jolly se encuentra bien. Sí, chicos estoy bien alegre voz baja. ¡Oh, alegre usted es nuestro amigo y héroe valiente.

UBesty, dijo que descansar un poco alegre. Jolly dijo que los chicos seguro, he salvado el mundo de Internet, y todos podemos acceder a Internet y los grupos sociales, sin tener miedo. Jolly venir a vernos en la escuela a veces. Yo USBesty haré, lo haré.